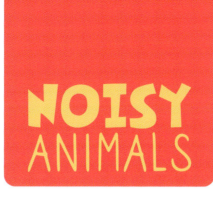

Say "Hi!" at the Seaside

By Madeline Tyler

www.littlebluehousebooks.com

Copyright © 2025 by Little Blue House, Mendota Heights, MN 55120. All rights reserved. No part of this book may be reproduced or utilized in any form or by any means without written permission from the publisher.

Little Blue House is distributed by North Star Editions: sales@northstareditions.com | 888-417-0195

Library of Congress Control Number: 2024936704

ISBN
979-8-89359-008-1 (hardcover)
979-8-89359-018-0 (paperback)
979-8-89359-038-8 (ebook pdf)
979-8-89359-028-9 (hosted ebook)

Printed in the United States of America
Mankato, MN
082024

Written by: Madeline Tyler

Edited by: Robin Twiddy

Designed by: Jasmine Pointer

QR by: Kelby Twyman

All facts, statistics, web addresses and URLs in this book were verified as valid and accurate at time of writing. No responsibility for any changes to external websites or references can be accepted by either the author or publisher.

To use the QR codes in this book, a grown-up will need to set one of these apps as the default browser on the device you are using:

- Chrome
- Safari
- Firefox
- Ecosia

Your QR app might open the links in this book right away. If it doesn't, tap the button that says "open," "continue," "browse," or something similar.

Image & Sound credits
All images courtesy of Shutterstock.com. With thanks to Getting Images, Thinkstock Photo, and iStockphoto.

All sounds (s) by http://soundbible.com. Character – Lorelyn Medina . Front Cover – Tartila, Maquiladora, Rvector. 3 – leolintang. 4 – Mike Koenig (s). 5 – curiosity. 6 – Nataliya Dorokhina, Daniel Simion (s).
7 – Mix3r. 8 – Willyam Bradberry. 9 – Maquiladora. 10 – Tim Zurowski, Mike Koenig. 11 – kateetc.
12 – Pinkcandy. 13 – intararit, Maquiladora. 14 – Roger de la Harpe. 15 – Maquiladora, intararit.
16 – Aleksandr Otopkov. 17 – Rvector, balyasina. 18 – Philip Pilosian, fws.gov (s). 20 – Daniel Huebner.
21 – Oceloti, Supreme Graphics. 22 – Chris Holman, National Park Servic (s).

Lots of animals live at the seaside. When people visit the seaside, it can get very noisy!

Scan the QR code to hear the noises of the seaside.

Seagulls eat fish and worms, but they sometimes steal chips and ice cream from people at the seaside.

Scan the QR code to hear the seagulls say "hi."

Eeyah!

Eeyah!

Eeyah!

A group of dolphins is called a pod. Dolphins like to swim and play together.

Can you say "hi" like a dolphin?

8

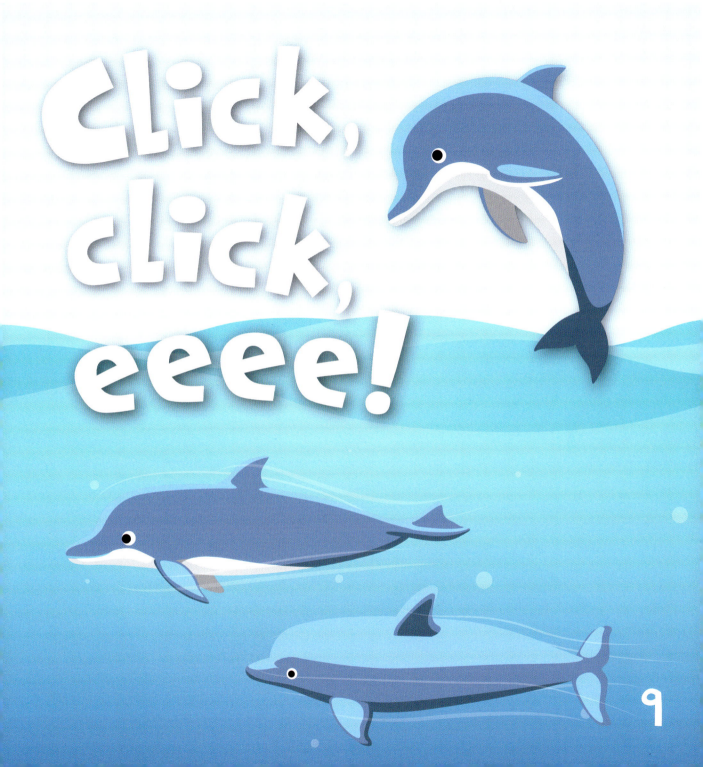

Seals are very good swimmers. They can hold their breath for 30 minutes or more, and some even sleep in the water.

Scan the QR code to hear the seal say "hi."

Donkeys are friendly animals and enjoy spending time with other donkeys.

Can you say "hi" like a donkey?

This pelican uses its large throat pouch to hold fish.

Scan the QR code to hear the pelican say "hi."

14

Crabs walk sideways along the beach.

Can you say "hi" like a crab?

A group of terns is called a colony. There can be up to 20,000 birds in a tern colony.

Scan the QR code to hear the terns say "hi."

Flying fish can use their fins to leap more than 3 feet (1 m) above the water.

Can you say "hi" like a flying fish?

20

Male humpback whales sing songs that can last for hours.

Scan the QR code to hear the humpback whales say "hi."

22